NATIONAL GEOGRAPHIC

The Civil War

Tim Paulsen

PICTURE CREDITS
Cover, page 30 (top) © Mort Kunstler, from the original painting "The Angle", © 1988 Mort Kunstler, Inc.; title page © James Schwabel/Panoramic Images; pages 2-3 © Smithsonian American Art Museum, Washington, D.C./Art Resource, NY; pages 4-5, 11 (bottom), 25 (top right), 34-b, 35-c illustrations by Rose Zgodzinski; pages 6 (top inset), 11 (top), 14 (right), 15 (center), 25 (bottom left), 26 (top), 31 (center), 34-a Courtesy Library of Congress; pages 6-7 (bottom), 12-13, 16-17, 21, 30 (bottom), 32, 34-f © Medford Historical Society Collection/CORBIS; pages 7 (top), 8, 10, 17-18 (inset), 21 (inset), 25 (top left), 28 (bottom), 34-d, 35-a © Bettmann/CORBIS; pages 9, 12 (top), 35-d © Scala/Art Resource, NY; pages 11 (top), 13 (top), 27, 31 (top), 35-e © CORBIS; pages 14 (center), 20, 23, 25 (bottom right), 26 (bottom), 31 (bottom), 34-c © The Granger Collection, New York; page 14 (left) © National Portrait Gallery, Smithsonian Institution/Art Resource, NY; page 15 (left) Courtesy of the National Archives; pages 15 (right), 35-b © Let us Have Peace by Jean Leon Jerome Ferris, Private Collection/Bridgeman Art Library; page 16 (inset bottom left) © Rare Book, Manuscript, and Special Collections Library, Duke University; pages 18, 22 © Tria Giovan/CORBIS; page 19 © Minnesota Historical Society/CORBIS; page 28 (top) © HIP/Scala/Art Resource, NY; page 29 (left and right) © Richard T. Nowitz/CORBIS; page 33 (left) *Blue or Gray?* by Kate Connell, © 2002 National Geographic Society, photo © Morton Kunstler; page 33 (center) *The Southeast* by Gare Thompson, © 2003 National Geographic Society, photo (top) © Bridgeman Art Library, (bottom) © Richard Cummins/CORBIS; page 33 (right) *The Emancipation Proclamation* by Marianne McComb, © 2004 National Geographic Society, photos © Getty Images; pages 34-e, 35-f © Philip Gould/CORBIS; page 36 © Richard T. Nowitz.

Produced through the worldwide resources of the National Geographic Society, John M. Fahey, Jr., President and Chief Executive Officer; Gilbert M. Grosvenor, Chairman of the Board; Nina D. Hoffman, Executive Vice President and President, Books and Education Publishing Group.

PREPARED BY NATIONAL GEOGRAPHIC SCHOOL PUBLISHING
Ericka Markman, Senior Vice President and President, Children's Books and Education Publishing Group; Steve Mico, Senior Vice President, Editorial Director, Publisher; Francis Downey, Executive Editor; Richard Easby, Editorial Manager; Anne Stone, Lori Dibble Collins, Editors; Bea Jackson, Director of Layout and Design; Jim Hiscott, Design Manager; Cynthia Olson, Art Director; Margaret Sidlosky, Illustrations Director; Matt Wascavage, Manager of Publishing Services; Sean Philpotts, Jane Ponton, Production Managers; Ted Tucker, Production Specialist.

MANUFACTURING AND QUALITY CONTROL
Christopher A. Liedel, Chief Financial Officer; Phillip L. Schlosser, Director; Clifton M. Brown III, Manager

CONSULTANT AND REVIEWER
Dr. Peter Hinks, Historian, Wethersfield, Connecticut

BOOK DESIGN/PHOTO RESEARCH
Steve Curtis Design, Inc.

◀ Soldiers rest after a battle.

Contents

Published by the National Geographic Society
1145 17th Street N.W.
Washington, D.C. 20036-4688

ISBN-10: 0-7922-5443-0
ISBN-13: 978-0-7922-5443-0

15 16 17 18 19 20 21 22
11 10 9 8 7 6 5 4

Printed in the USA.

Build **Background**

What Is a

People have fought wars throughout history. Some wars are fought between countries. Some wars are between people of the same country. These wars are called **civil wars.**

In the mid 1800s, a terrible civil war was fought in the United States. Eleven states in the South broke away from the rest of the country. They wanted to create a new country. The states in the North fought the states in the South for four long years.

civil war – a conflict in which two groups in the same country fight for control of that country

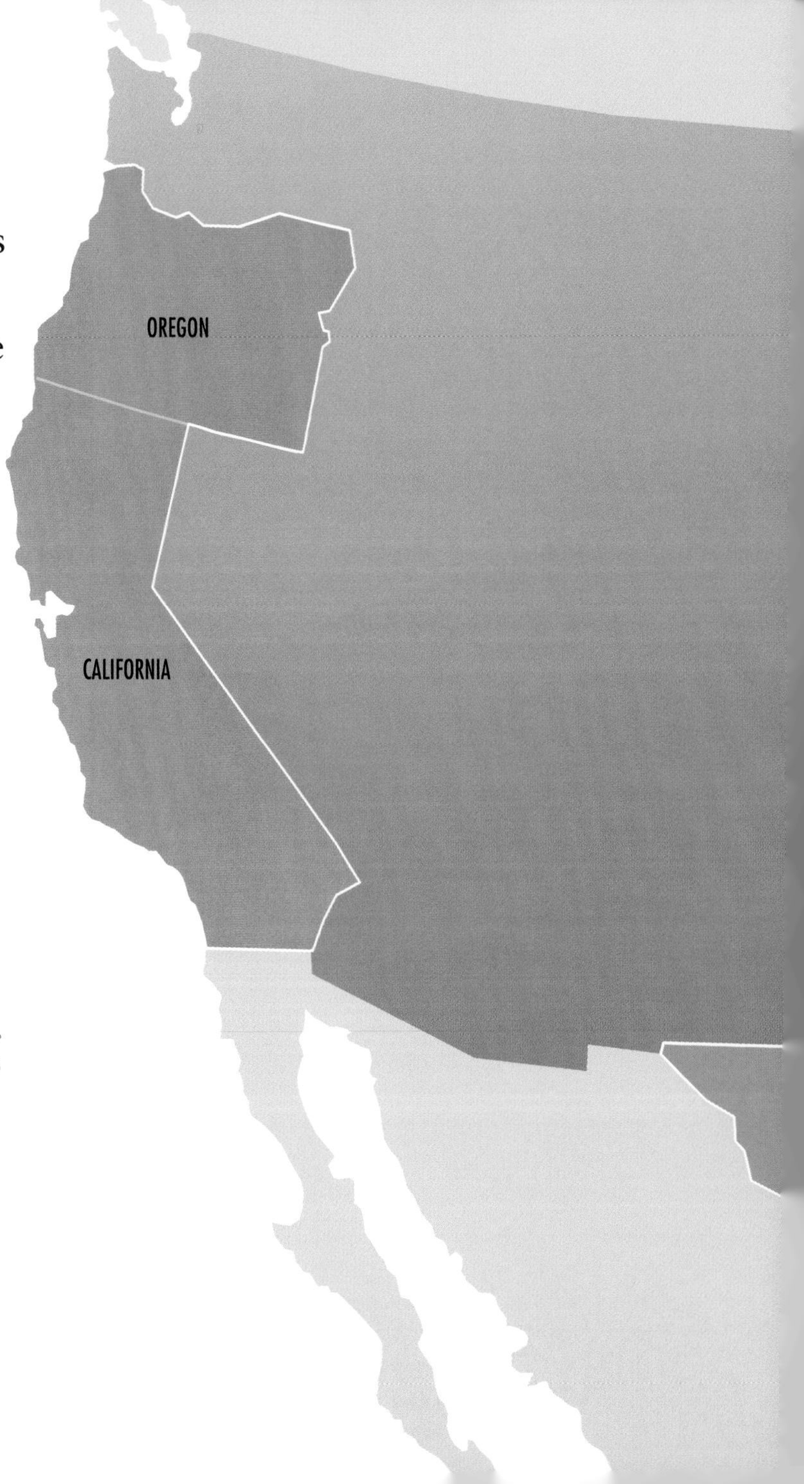

Civil War?

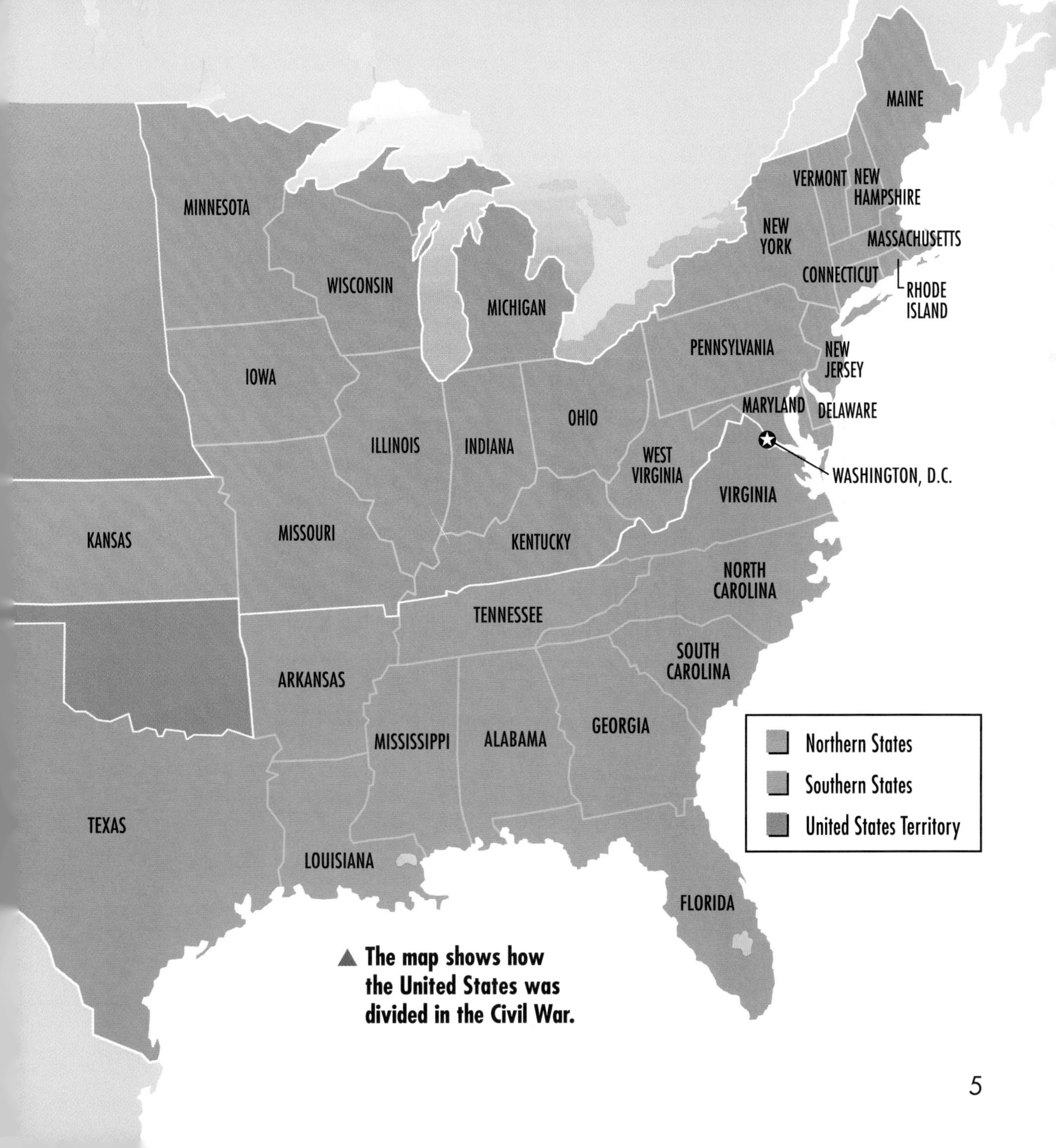

▲ **The map shows how the United States was divided in the Civil War.**

1 Understand the **Big Idea**

Big Idea
From 1861 to 1865, a war divided the United States.

Set Purpose
Find out about the events that led to the Civil War.

THE A

▲ Many people died in the Civil War.

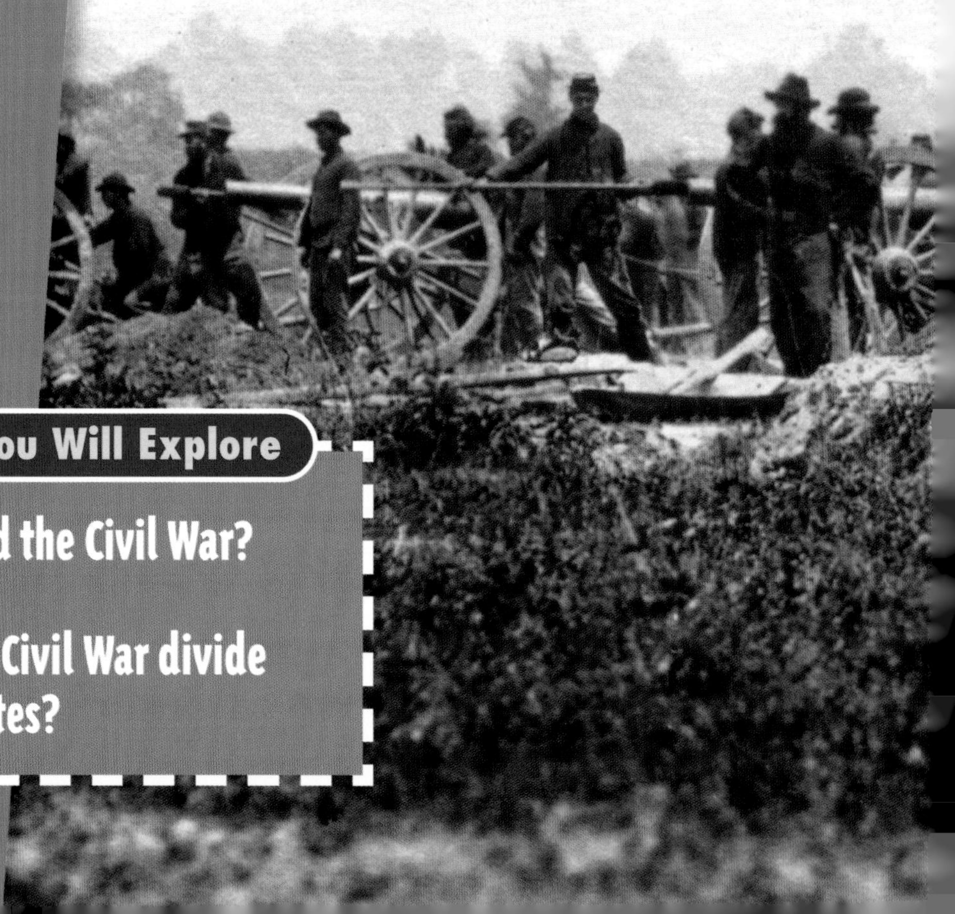

Questions You Will Explore

What caused the Civil War?

How did the Civil War divide the United States?

MERICAN Civil War

The Civil War was fought by Americans on American soil. Men of all ages fought. Grandfathers fought. Teenage boys fought. About 620,000 people lost their lives in the Civil War.

▲ These southern soldiers await a battle with northern troops.

Southern Farms

In the 1800s, a lot of people in the North and South had different ideas. For example, many people had different ideas about **slavery.** Slavery is when one person owns another and forces him or her to work.

Most whites in the South believed slavery was right. They kept slaves to work for them on their farms. They thought it would be hard to run their farms without slaves.

slavery – when one person owns another person

▼ **Slaves worked in the cotton fields around the time of the Civil War.**

Northern Factories

There were more factories in the North than in the South. People worked in the factories for pay. Many people in the North felt that slavery was wrong. Slavery was against the law in most of the North.

People in both the North and the South had strong **opinions** about slavery. After many years, these differences led to war.

opinion – a belief or point of view

▼ **People in the North built many factories like these.**

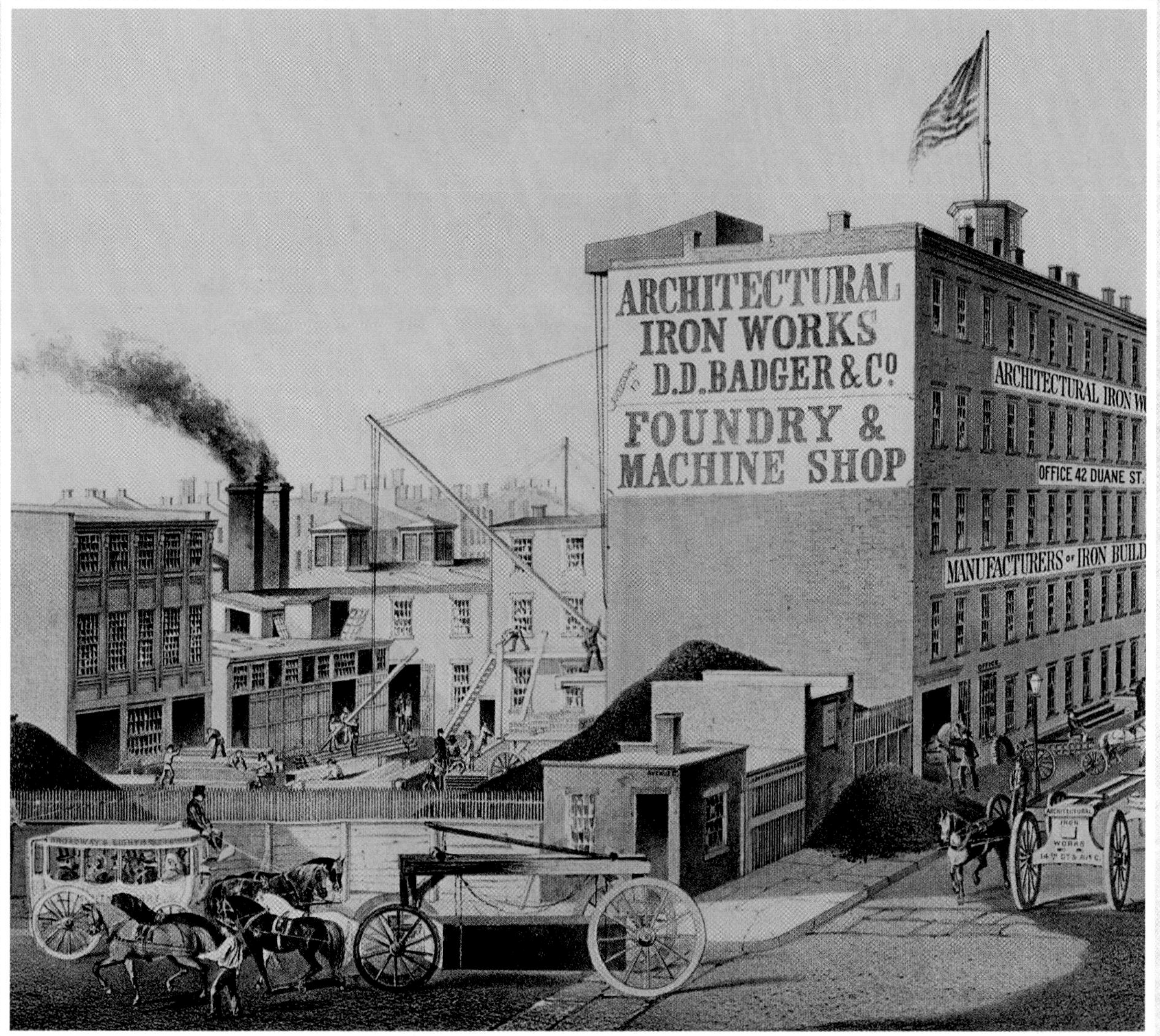

A New President

Abraham Lincoln was elected President in 1860. Lincoln did not support slavery. People in the North were happy Lincoln was elected.

In the South, however, many people were not happy. Some Southerners feared that Lincoln planned to end slavery. They decided to **secede,** or break away, from the United States. They wanted to form a separate country.

secede – to break away from

▼ **Abraham Lincoln became President of the United States in 1861.**

A Country Divides in Two

In all, eleven states seceded. These southern states started a new country. They called it the Confederate States of America, or the **Confederacy.** The Confederacy elected its own President. His name was Jefferson Davis.

The states that remained were still the United States of America. They were called the **Union.** Abraham Lincoln was its President.

Confederacy – the states that seceded from the United States during the Civil War

Union – the states that remained with the United States during the Civil War

▼ **Jefferson Davis was President of the Confederacy.**

▼ **Eleven states seceded from the United States.**

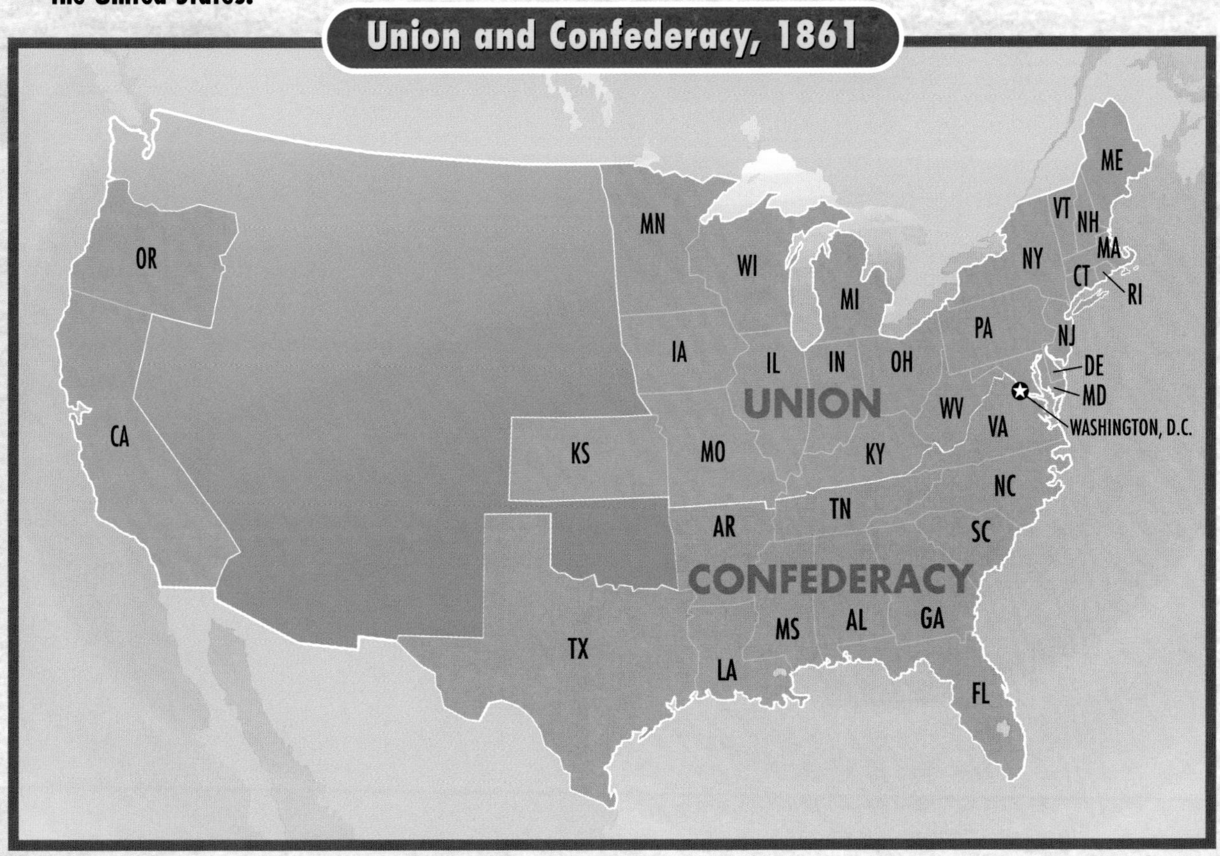

The Civil War Begins

President Lincoln did not want war. He told the nation, "There needs to be no bloodshed or **violence.**" But there was.

On April 12, 1861, Confederates fired on Union soldiers at Fort Sumter in South Carolina. The Union soldiers quickly gave up. The Confederacy had its first **victory.** The Civil War had begun.

violence – an action that destroys things or injures people

victory – a win

▼ **The Confederates started the war when they attacked Fort Sumter.**

Fighting the War

The fighting damaged homes, towns, and families. Land everywhere became battlefields. Some cities were burned to the ground.

Churches and schoolhouses became hospitals for wounded soldiers. Thousands of men died.

▼ **A nurse cares for two Union soldiers in a hospital during the Civil War.**

▼ **Much of Richmond, Virginia, was destroyed during the Civil War.**

Life Changes With War

For the people left at home, life was hard. Women and children worked on the farms. They also made supplies for soldiers at war. Many families lost fathers, sons, or brothers in battles.

Much of the war was fought in the South. War became a part of daily life for families in the South. Some families were told to leave their homes so soldiers could work and live in them. Cities, such as Atlanta, were burned to the ground.

A Civil War Time Line

1860

Abraham Lincoln is elected President.

Southern states begin to secede.

1861

Jefferson Davis becomes President of the Confederacy.

The Confederates attack Fort Sumter. The Civil War begins.

1862

Black soldiers begin to fight in the Union Army.

A Four-Year War

The Civil War was fought for four long years. Both sides fought hard. The soldiers and the people suffered.

Finally, on April 9, 1865, the South **surrendered.** The South's leaders said they would stop fighting. The North had won the war.

surrender – to give up

Stop and Think!

What events led to the Civil War?

1863	1864	1865
Lincoln's Emancipation Proclamation frees all slaves in the Confederacy.	**The Union wins a victory in Atlanta, Georgia. Atlanta is destroyed.** **Lincoln is reelected.**	**The Confederacy surrenders.**

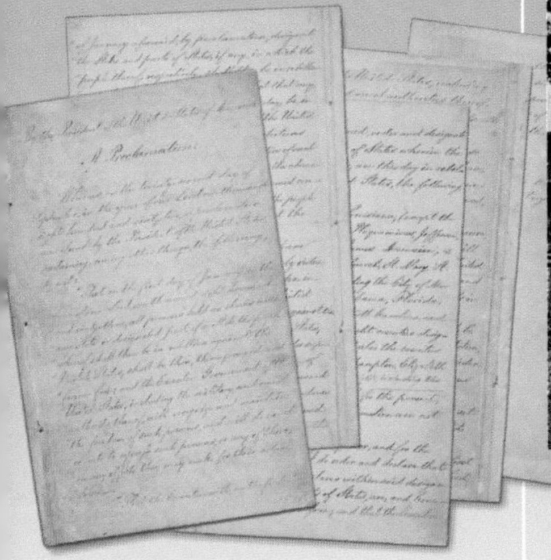

2 Take a Closer Look

Recap

Explain how the Civil War divided the United States.

Set Purpose

Read to learn how the Civil War affected a girl living in the South.

THE WAR

AT HOME

ADAPTED FROM A REAL CIVIL WAR DIARY

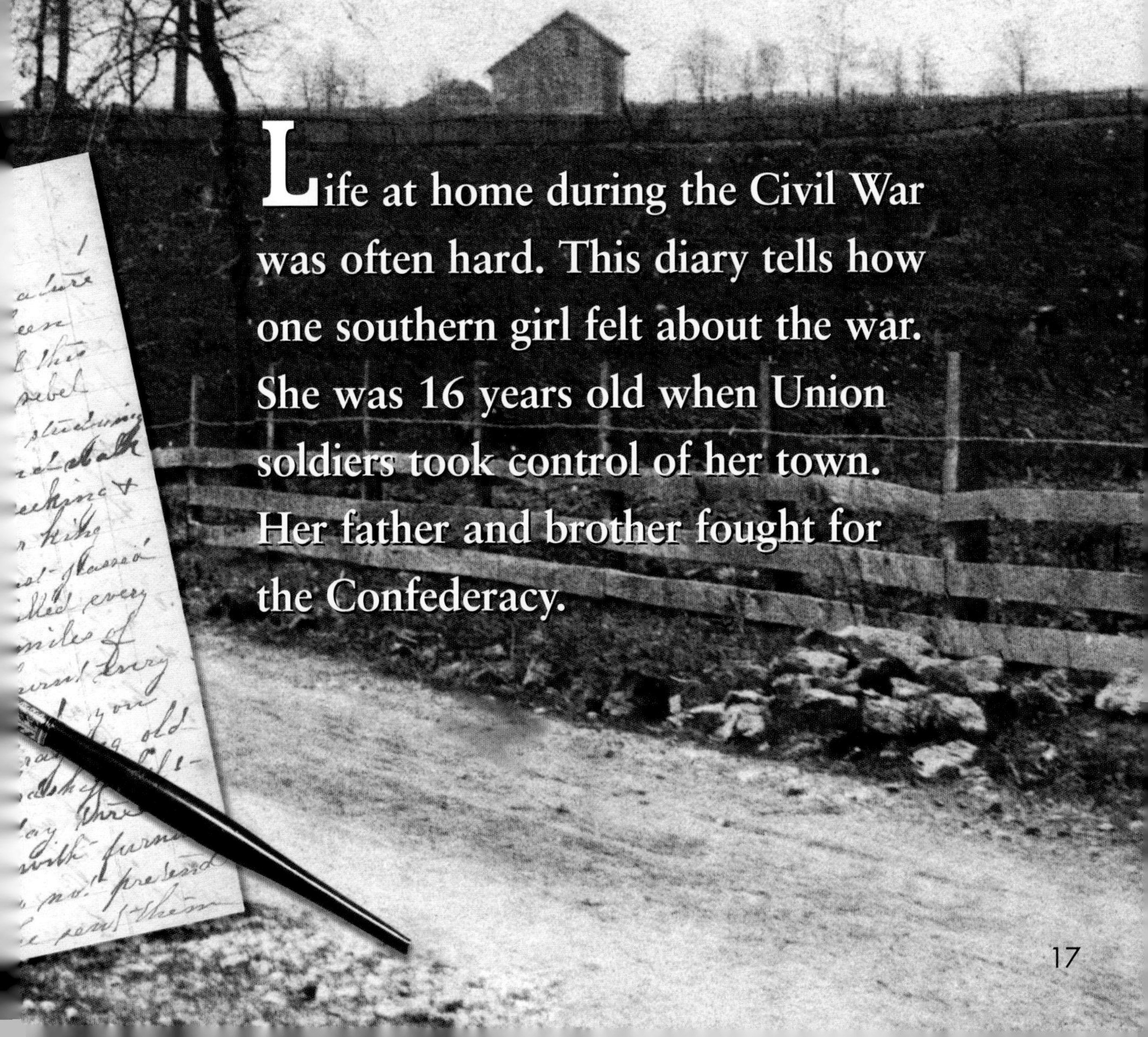

Life at home during the Civil War was often hard. This diary tells how one southern girl felt about the war. She was 16 years old when Union soldiers took control of her town. Her father and brother fought for the Confederacy.

YANKEES IN GALLATIN

April 2, 1864 Today **Yankee** troops marched into town. The Union troops will rule us like they were kings. I sure wish Pa was here. Or my brother Joe. They would show the Yanks a thing or two.

April 8, 1864 Some Yanks took Pa's horse today. They said it was theirs. We all know that is a lie, but what can we do?

April 14, 1864 Today I heard some Yank officers down at the square. They were talking about bushwhackers. Bushwhacking is what the **Rebels** are doing to the Yankees. Our men attack at night or surprise the Yanks from behind. That is bushwhacking.

The Yanks say it will go hard if they catch the bushwhackers. I worry about Joe and hope he is not one of them. Or if he is, I pray he will not get caught.

Yankee – a soldier for the North during the Civil War

Rebel – a soldier for the South during the Civil War

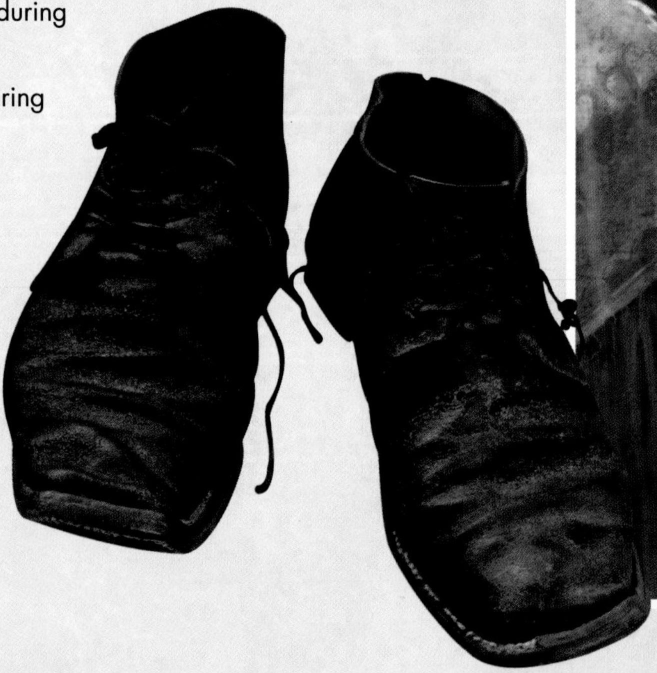

▶ **These boots were worn by a Civil War soldier.**

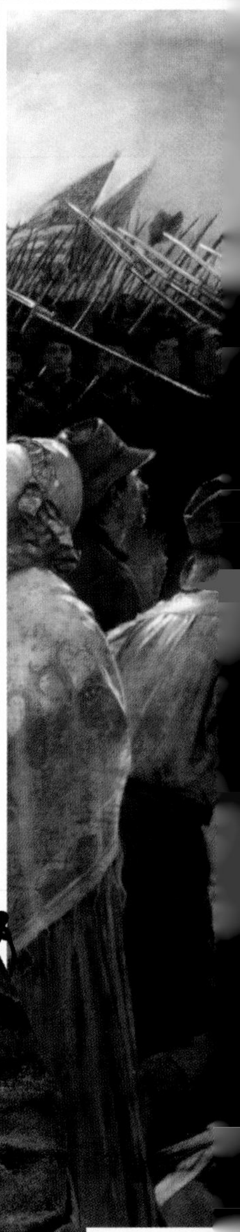

May 1, 1864 This is the dullest May-day holiday ever. Usually May-day is a fun time. The whole town comes out to celebrate spring. Not this year, though.

All of the men are gone to fight. Those of us left do not have much to celebrate. The good news is the Yanks do not seem to be having any fun, either.

▼ **Yankee soldiers march through the South.**

LIFE CHANGES

May 3, 1864 The Yankee troops set free all the slaves in east Tennessee! Gallatin is filling up with "**freedmen.**" They are freed slaves.

May 9, 1864 There is a new school in town. The Yankees built it to teach freed slaves in. Now I might work there. Ma says we need the money.

May 16, 1864 The Yankee schoolteacher is not so bad. I even shared my pencils with a freed slave girl named Swanda.

freedman – a freed slave

▼ **Freedmen attend their own school.**

May 20, 1864 I had to do work at home today. Me and Ma do all of the stuff Pa and Joe used to do. Ma says the Yankees have been behaving badly again. Best for us to stay near home and get some work done.

May 29, 1864 Yanks showed up and wanted lunch. We gave it to them. They ate just about everything in sight. I thought they would never leave, but finally they did. They took our best sofa and two chairs with them! Ma said to be quiet. We are lucky they did not hurt us.

▼ **Soldiers sit in a Union camp.**

WAR IN THE BACKYARD

June 10, 1864 There are many Yanks in the area. They are camped in the woods in front of us. They have already paid us several visits. They killed sheep, goats, and chickens. Our Yankees are not very neighborly! Some came today and demanded their dinner at two o'clock. We did not give it to them. We do not have much food left.

July 13, 1864 The war came almost to our backyard yesterday! The Yanks chased some bushwhackers into our neighbor's barn. I took some milk and cereal out to them before the shooting started.

July 26, 1864 Word came that my brother Joe was captured. Yanks took him to a prison in Indiana. It is called Camp Morton. Joe was not with the bushwhackers. They say he will be okay. He is still a prisoner of war, though. I am worried about him.

▲ **A Union leader's hat**

July 31, 1864 Got a letter from Joe! He is sad, but says he is treated okay. Still no word on Pa. We think he is fighting out east.

August 14, 1864 Heard there is bad fighting in Atlanta. That is in Georgia. Everyone says it hurts our cause. How I wish this war would end.

▼ **Union soldiers take prisoners during the Civil War.**

Stop and Think!

HOW did the Civil War change life for people at home?

3 Make **Connections**

Recap

Explain how the Civil War changed the United States and its people.

Set Purpose

Read to learn more about the Civil War.

CONNECT WHAT YOU HAVE LEARNED

The Civil War

Wars between people in the same country are called civil wars. Americans fought a civil war from 1861 to 1865.

Here are some ideas that you learned about the Civil War.

- Before the Civil War, many Southerners owned slaves.
- Eleven southern states broke away from the United States and formed the Confederacy.
- The Confederate states and the United States fought the Civil War.
- The Civil War ended slavery.

Check What You Have Learned

Why did the southern states break away from the United States?

▲ Many Southerners owned slaves.

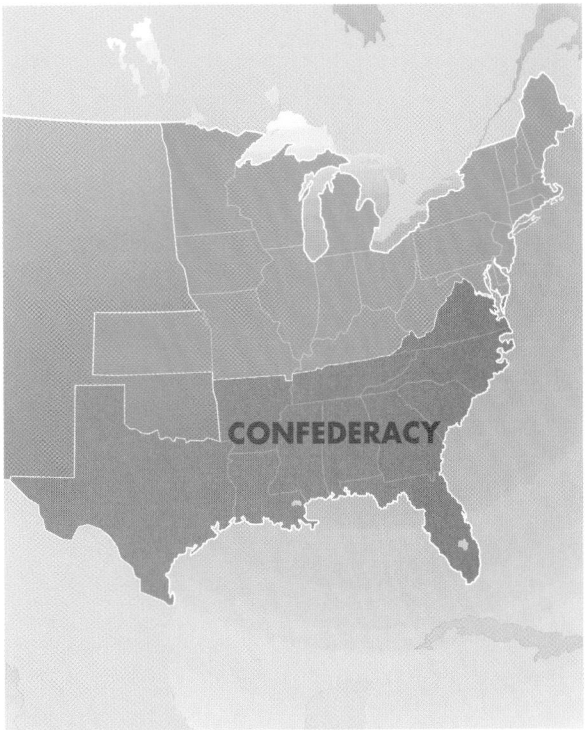

▲ Eleven states formed the Confederacy.

▲ The Civil War was fought from 1861 to 1865.

▲ The Civil War brought an end to slavery.

▲ **Clara Barton helped many soldiers who were hospitalized during the Civil War.**

Clara Barton

Clara Barton was a Union Army nurse. She worked very close to the fighting. During one battle a bullet went through her sleeve. Then it killed the man she was treating!

Clara Barton later started the American Red Cross. It helps people who are hurt in war. It also helps people who are hurt by disasters.

Children of War

Young people worked hard during the Civil War. Often, 15-year-old boys served in the army. Some soldiers were even younger!

Very young boys served as drummer boys. Their drums helped soldiers on the battlefield know what to do. A certain beat might mean march or charge. Boys also played horns to wake up soldiers.

▶ **This African-American child was a drummer boy in the Civil War.**

Greenbacks

Did you know that the use of paper money in the United States began during the Civil War? Before that time, the government paid for items with gold. But banks began to run out of gold during the war.

In 1862, the government began printing paper money to use instead of gold. The bills were printed on only one side with green ink. People called them “greenbacks.” They became very popular.

▼ This 1862 greenback was worth ten cents.

▲ This 1896 greenback was worth one dollar. It shows Martha Washington and George Washington.

CONNECT TO TODAY

Civil War Reenactments

Across America, special groups act out, or reenact, Civil War battles and events. Most of these groups use uniforms, guns, and tools that are just like what Civil War soldiers used. People also camp in tents and eat foods that the soldiers ate. Modern clothes and tools are not allowed.

◀ **People reenact events from the Civil War.**

Extend
Learning

Zoom in on Words

Many kinds of words are used in this book. Here you will learn about contractions. You will also learn about compound words.

Contractions

A contraction is a shortened form of two words. It is made by leaving out some letters and adding an apostrophe. What contractions do you already know?

he is = he's

We think **he's** fighting out east.

do not = don't

The Yanks **don't** seem to be having any fun.

Compound Words

A compound word is made by joining two shorter words. You can often figure out what a compound word means by knowing what the two shorter words mean.

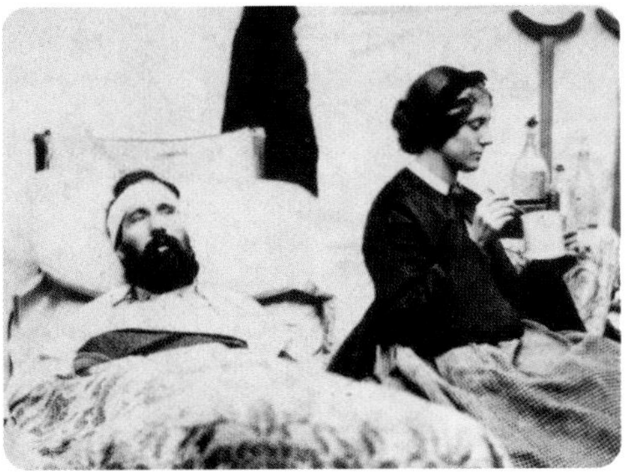

blood + shed = bloodshed

There was a lot of **bloodshed** during the battle.

battle + field = battlefield

Soldiers fought on the **battlefield.**

freed + men = freedmen

Many **freedmen** went to school.

Research and Write

Write About the Civil War

Find out more about important battles that happened during the Civil War. Look for details about who won and where they were fought. How do these battles fit into the time line on pages 14 and 15?

Research
Collect books and reference materials, or go online.

Read and Take Notes
As you read, take notes and draw pictures.

Write
Write an informational report about one or more important battles.

Read and Compare

Read More About the Civil War

Find and read other books about the Civil War and the North and South. As you read, think about these questions.

- What do these books have in common with *The Civil War?*
- Why was life hard for southern families during the Civil War?
- How did the Civil War change the United States?

Books to Read

▲ **Find out more about the Civil War.**

▲ **Discover the history and culture of the southeastern United States.**

▲ **Learn more about Abraham Lincoln and the Emancipation Proclamation.**

Glossary

KEY CONCEPT

civil war (page 4)
A conflict in which two groups in the same country fight for control of that country
From 1861 to 1865, the Civil War was fought in the United States.

KEY CONCEPT

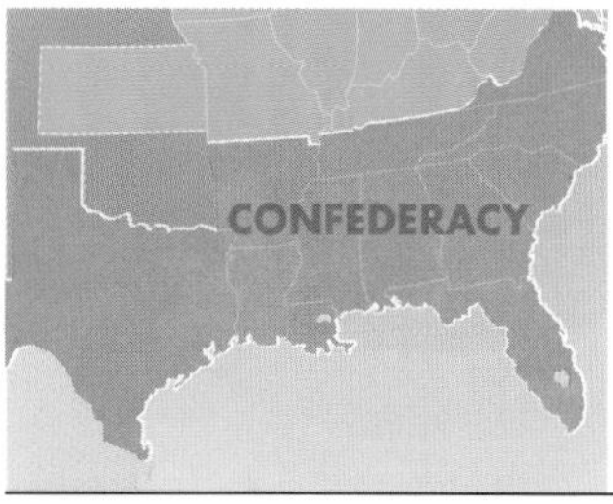

Confederacy (page 11)
The states that seceded from the United States during the Civil War
The southern states were called the Confederacy.

freedman (page 20)
A freed slave
Freedmen went to their own schools.

opinion (page 9)
A belief or point of view
People in both the North and the South had strong opinions about slavery.

Rebel (page 18)
A soldier for the South during the Civil War
Southern soldiers were called Rebels.

KEY CONCEPT

secede (page 10)
To break away from
The southern states decided to secede from the United States.

KEY CONCEPT

slavery (page 8)
When one person owns another person
Most people in the South believed slavery was right.

surrender (page 15)
To give up
The southern states surrendered in 1865.

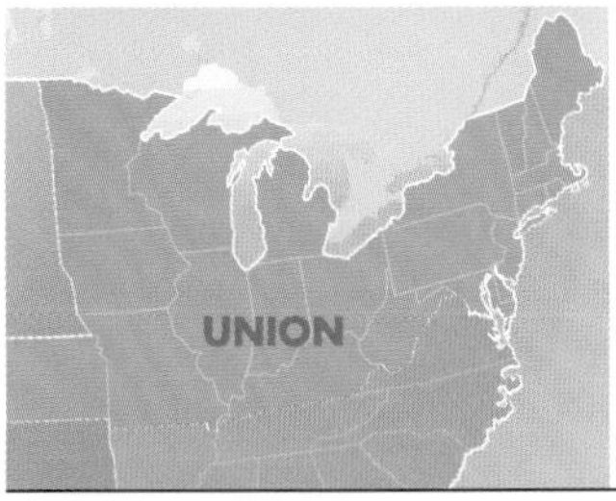

KEY CONCEPT

Union (page 11)
The states that remained with the United States during the Civil War
Abraham Lincoln was President of the Union.

victory (page 12)
A win
The Confederacy had its first victory at Fort Sumter.

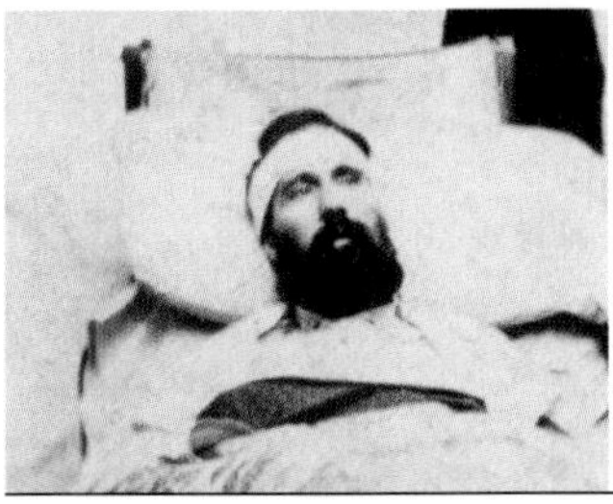

violence (page 12)
An action that destroys things or injures people
The President did not want bloodshed or violence.

Yankee (page 18)
A soldier for the North during the Civil War
The Union troops were called Yankees.

Index